HOW TO BE HUMAN

Diary of an Autistic Girl
By Florida Frenz

Foreword

Not too long ago, my friend and I had a discussion about which was worse, anorexia or autism. She argued anorexia was worse because it can kill you. At the time, I couldn't come up with a good enough rebuttal, so the discussion ended.

Snort feels like snot in your nose.

Now I have the perfect answer. Anorexia is caused by traumatic life experiences as well as messages from society and media. In other words, anorexia comes from the nurturing anorexics receive, not from their natural dispositions. However, for autistics like me, it's in our nature to be this way. Autism is not the result of a chemical imbalance, but rather a difference in the physical structure of the brain and the way its neurons connect together. Anorexia is like a software problem in the brain, whereas autism is like a hardware problem. Though for autism, you can't just go to the computer store and pick up another brain. You just rely on the brain's ability to form new connections, changing its structure to resemble that of a normal person's. That's no easy feat, and it gets harder as we grow older and our brains lose plasticity. The autism must be addressed before too many humans make the autistic person feel like planet earth is the worst planet they could have accidentally landed on.

Snap feels like pushing soapy plates together.

Lighting feels like being really, really shocked.

The world revolves around principles you just can't grasp. At school, students whisper and giggle. Even when the teacher silences them, nothing is silent like you would reasonably expect it to be. The students still create noise by shifting positions in their seats, which makes their pants rustle and their chairs squeak.

The teacher can be just as noisy, pounding away on a laptop, turning the pages in a book, and occasionally clomping around the classroom.

Your ears aren't the only sense being bombarded. Tiny fonts lead your eyes astray, so you can never find the correct line to start reading from. Perfumes cause your nose to stuff up. The texture of clothing on your skin or an unexpected touch from another person feels like someone dropped a slimy eel on you.

The worst part about this is that the more it happens, the more it bothers you. Those yucky sensations don't leave your body as soon as you stop getting exposed to them, but instead continue echoing through your nervous system, jarring every cell in your body. The more you get exposed to, the stronger the echoes are, and the less tolerant you are. It becomes a perpetual trap of sensory overload.

On top of that, or maybe because of it, falling asleep and staying asleep can be very hard. It can really put you in a nasty mood because A) you're tired and B) it's unpredictable when you'll have a good or bad night.

Cat Hissing

feels like being furios and scared at the same time.

Dish Washer

feels like having a big gush of water on you.

outside
inside

And those are just the physical challenges of being autistic. The core of the problem lies in the brain and how it understands your own emotions as well as those of others. The main problem is, it doesn't. Our brains were built to understand concepts that can be broken down into logical pieces, or chains of rationale. For example, most of us understand math facts well because the steps used to get the answer are either right or wrong. The answer only means what you have at the end. If you solve the problem, whats 1 + 1,

Foot Steps

feels like clapping.

the answer is two. Therefore the answer can only mean two, and there's no way it can mean three, four, or five. Also, the cause and effect on other numbers is clear. Add two to a number, and you get that number plus two. Subtract two from a number, you get that number minus two. Divide a number by two, you get half of that number. All of that is unambiguous.

My Dream Room

Emotions can be broken down into logical pieces most of the time, but what's hard to grasp is the cause and effect relationship that comes with the emotion. When a person is sad (the cause), they might cry, listen to slow, soft music, contact friends as an effect of the sadness. It's a bit more complicated than simply subtracting two, isn't it? Still, there are even more complicated situations than that, such as looking at an effect and guessing what emotion caused it. Then, there's the ability to do that for the feelings of others. Honestly, don't you think all those normal people do emotional calculus every day without realizing it?

Button to change background.

Aww! I love the forest look!.

A watch that's a time Machine

Time Machine Dreamland Dinosaur 1:48 PM

Then, as if dealing with autism weren't hard enough, there's one misconception that many normal people believe, and they can brainwash you into believing it too -- that autistics are only interested in ourselves and the universe we inhabit inside of our head.

A paint brush that does what you want but never messes up!

Really, we are interested in others, and we do want to inhabit the same universe as everyone else. However, because of what I said earlier, we have trouble doing either. Retreating into our heads is our only respite from the constant chaos. We stay in our heads because it's so much simpler than venturing out.

When we finally take the initiative to try, it's often hard to function on a basic level because we are constantly being flooded with sensory info. Plus we were so busy being overwhelmed by emotions and sensations in the past, we didn't have the space in our brains to absorb knowledge on how to interact with others, so we aren't very good at it.

A machine that makes you fly now you have a lot of extra time because it goes so fast.

For these reasons, often the attempt to socialize becomes uncomfortable for both the autistic and the regular person. Basically, we autistics are poorly rewarded for a task that is very hard, so we avoid doing it. In this way, autistics are the same as humans.

It's a lot to ask, but if autistics want to be part of this world, they have to be stronger than most people. There were many times I would have preferred doodling to hanging out with my friends. Moments when I couldn't concentrate on a task or interact with others because the place was too loud or busy. Moments when I wished I had no emotions because processing them and swinging between highs and lows was so draining.

A bath tub that is like the spa massage and the ocean combined.

Truthfully, I still have those moments. Even as I sit here now, I can hear the high-pitched hum of my Dad's aquarium pump which is rubbing my inner-ear hairs the wrong way. I've just learned to cope over many years. Not that learning to cope was easy, but I saw it was the only way to succeed. Once you learn to cope, the brain doesn't feel the need to create its own universe, and it has much more free space to learn about social skills. Only when I gained social skills and therefore effective means to communicate with others, was I able to gain some control over my surroundings and tell people what they could do to accomodate my autism. Even if that meant something as small as telling the other person to call me back in five minutes when I could put myself in a quieter spot.

A security camera that shoots lasers at unwanted visitors

Learning how to communicate allowed me to understand how normal brains work, which let me see that even if we were from different planets, we had a lot in common. Some of those normal people even had the ability to explain how emotions work in a way that my logical brain could comprehend. To achieve all of this, I've probably had to work harder in fifteen years than some people do in their whole lives.

I'd have my own zoo full of cool animals

It's been worth it, because though I'm autistic, it no longer defines who I am. I have become an empowered autistic.
To the other autistics out there, I know you can become empowered as well. You've just got to give your brain the right tools to reconfigure its hardware. You'll become a brilliant brain engineer that may even invent replacement brains for autistics, which really could be sold to them at the computer store. But only if they want it.
They might be perfectly happy with what they have. After so many years of hard work, I am.

Magic brush that grants you any hairstyle!

A machine that'd let me get sucked into any computer or videogames.

I dedicate this book to my parents.
I must thank them for always encouraging me to learn more and strive higher.
Yet I'm also glad they didn't expect me to do it alone
and have always been there to help.
Mom and Dad, I just want to let you know
that unless you'd instilled those lessons in me,
I don't think I would have ever tried to make this book.

Step 1: Figure Out Faces

Adults would grab my face and tell me to look them in their eyes, but one day I got the good advice to start by looking in the general direction of their faces. Once you do that, it's easier to see their expressions.

I did this picture on facial expressions when I was a seven- or eight-year-old. The world is hard to understand if you can't read the faces of other people.

It's like being in a **foreign country** and not understanding the **language**, except worse, because your parents, family, friends, and teachers are fluent in it.

When you don't get facial expressions, you feel like a real idiot, or like you were mistakenly   placed

on

the

wrong

planet.

Happy about getting new glasses

Sad about being teased about new glasses

Mad that someone would ever offend his glasses!

The right one being where the inhabitants communicate with spoken language and **tentacles**, not their faces.

When you finally identify the facial expressions and what they mean, you experience an immense **feeling of relief** because you realize that even if you are living on the wrong planet, you have the **talent** and **resources** to adjust to it.

Step 2: Figure Out Feelings
(your own first of all)

Once you actually look at people's faces, you have to figure out what all those **movements** and **contortions** mean. But before you can figure that out, you have to understand how **you** feel.

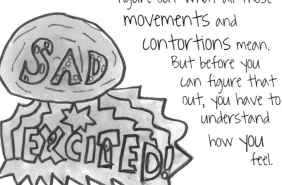

I drew this back in second grade, I was having a lot of trouble **expressing** or even **understanding** my feelings. By drawing different words that showed emotion and by giving them **colors**,

textures,

and *illustrations*,

I began to define my emotions in a way I could **understand.**

At last, I could possess some idea as to what I was **feeling** and tell it to other people.

Step 3: Match the Feelings to the Faces

If you don't know how you are feeling on the inside, then what you show on the outside might not match, and then you really look like alien.

Outside good day

Inside on a good day

See how the faces look the same on a good day as on a bad day -- what's the difference here?

How would you know?

Outside on a bad day

Inside on a bad day

Step 4: Figure Out Fake Feelings

It's one thing to read real emotions on faces, but figuring out fake ones is a huge challenge! How do humans know a smile isn't real? How can they tell pretend crying? This was like calculus or advanced astrophysics to me!

Public Face

Very happy and nice.

Inner face

Feeling very unloved and jelous of others.

Public Face

No one likes me they hate me!

Inner face

Soon I'll have all the toys in the world hee hee!

Even after I learned about the different facial expressions, I still believed that whatever emotion a person's face showed must be what he or she felt. My therapist Shelah made me draw this picture so that I'd know that people can manipulate their faces for personal gain or to hide unwanted feelings and secrets. I learned about deceit by drawing this picture. Now I could convince most of the world I was still guileless while I was a cunning mastermind just by manipulating my face. BWHAHA!!!

Step 5: What Kind of Human Are You?

What kind of human do you want to be? Do you want to be something that pleases **yourself** or do you just want to look good to **other** people?

As an eight-year-old, I wanted so badly to be **included** with my friends that I would blindly follow them wherever they went without consulting my **conscience**. I would often dash out of sight without telling the adult responsible for me where I was going, and sometimes when I was with one particular friend, she would persuade me to knock on the doors of complete strangers!

Which one of you should I listen to?

Take pizza to choir and chuck it at everyone

Don't do that it's not right!

Fortunately, nothing bad ever came of me those times when I **ignored** my conscience, but clearly I needed to learn how to listen to it. All the other drawings in this book helped me **understand** the world, but this one made me realize that understanding would be **worthless** unless I could use it to make my own choices. Since I now possessed this understanding, I also possessed the responsibility of using it to protect my physical safety as well as my budding **individuality.**

Step 6: How Do You Decide to Act?

By listening to humans or to yourself? Whose voice really matters? Once I started making friends, this was really complicated. I wasn't sure how to stand up for myself. . .or even if I should.

At age eight, I was nervous that I would get bullied. To address my nerves, Shelah suggested I draw this picture so that I could brainstorm options for what to do in a situation where someone dared to insult or bully me.

Step 7: Figure Out Behavior AND Emotions

Because I like things to be measured and logical, charts help a lot. I used this one to figure out how bad something really was before I reacted.

Kid Meter of bad behavior

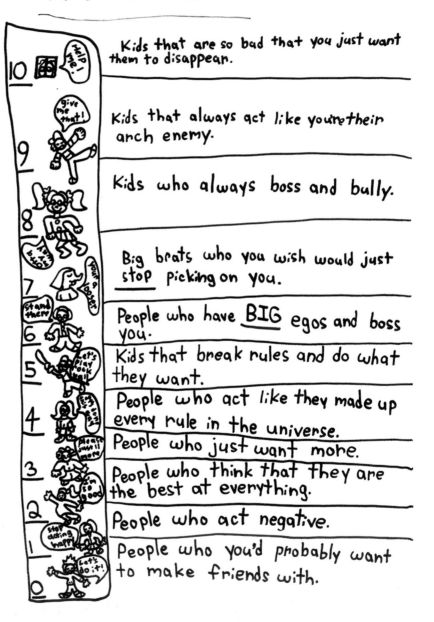

This chart helped me **identify** who would make a bad friend, but it also helped to show me that if a person was a 1 or 2 on the meter, he or she could still make a pretty good **friend**. Friends are only **human** and they will have their faults, which was a concept the alien within me disliked vehemently, but eventually **accepted**.

10 — Kids that are so bad that you just want them to disappear.

9 — Kids that always act like you're their arch enemy.

8 — Kids who always boss and bully.

7 — Big brats who you wish would just **stop** picking on you.

6 — People who have **BIG** egos and boss you.

5 — Kids that break rules and do what they want.

4 — People who act like they made up every rule in the universe.

People who just want more.

3 — People who think that they are the best at everything.

2 — People who act negative.

1 — People who you'd probably want to make friends with.

0

I did this chart inspired by the Amelia Books by Marissa Moss. It helped me attach **words** and **emotions** together so I could express myself better and think about what part of the chart I was on during any given day. It was like an **emotional thermometer**.

	You're super happy, you feel like with one leap you could reach the stars!
	You're very happy but you feel like something is holding you back from having the best day in your life.
	You're happy but in an avarage way.
	Today hasn't been good but it hasn't been bad either, from this point it could go either way.
	you're a bit mad like when you spill some on your shirt but it dosen't ruin your day.
	You're mad but in a medium way not in a big way.
	You're now sad now this could just reck the whole day.
	You're abousitly furios this defenitly recks the day!
	You feel that this day is the worst in your life. No matter what, nothing can cheer you up you feel like a mound of dirt!

Step 8: Avoid the Perfection Trap

Now that you're close to human, the alien may still want to be perfect.

I've always been a perfectionist but back when I was eight that manifested itself a lot of the time as wanting to behave perfectly and getting frustrated when I couldn't. Shelah was trying to show me that kids who seemed to behave perfectly really weren't as perfect as I imagined them to be.

I didn't believe her, so she made me draw a kid with perfect behavior. I saw what she meant afterwards. If I really acted like the kid I'd drawn, every other child in the world would've had every right to sneak into my bedroom in the middle of the night and graffiti my walls with "Tattle Tale" and "Bigmouth".

When I was younger, anything bad that happened would automatically ruin my whole day. By creating this picture, I realized most of the bad things that happened to me fit under the "Small Bad Things" category, so even though part of my day had been rotten, the rest of it still had the potential to be good. "Big Bad Things" were still extremely rotten, but they became more tolerable because I realized in all probability, I would have a better day tomorrow. So then I'd listen to some music, imagine that I had the world's best singing voice, and pretend to be a little orphan called Annie.

Small Bad Things

Throwing things away that could be rycicled

Ac sadentle 4 clicking out of the screen.

Boogers in nose.

Tarring roof outside choir practice

Medium Bad things

Skipping a few hours of sleep because of pictures.

Getting toothpaste on your shirt.

Having a bad day at classes

Having to do homework

Bad, Bad Things

Opposit sexes kissing each other. Except for parents.

Getting into trouble.

Beliving your older friend that it's okay to knock on strangers doors.

Step 9: Best Friend Envy

The best part of being human is making friends. But before you can have a good friend you need to learn how to be a good friend.

When I was eight, I wanted to be best friends with a girl, but she already had a best friend. I was wondering why I wasn't that girl's best friend. This was a way for me to explore what qualities I needed to be a best friend. I know that people who meet me now may find it hard to believe but back then, I really had to work hard to be a good friend.

Step 10: How to be a Friend, How NOT to be one

Don't get **trapped** into a bad friendship just because you want a friend. First figure out whether that person is a good friend for you.

By drawing this, I became more **conscious** of how I behaved around my friends and started to avoid accidentally doing the things listed. At least that's what I thought when I looked at it, but Shelah just reminded me that actually it was a lesson on **perspective** taking, that not everybody is going to be nice to me so I should choose my friends **wisely**.

Step 11: How to Handle Enemies

Being human means that you have enemies as well as friends. At least I did, and I had to figure out how to handle them without getting in trouble in the human world.

Voodoo Doll for Your Enemies

Poke here for brain surgery

Poke here for earwax problems

Poke here for lice

Poke here for butter fingures

Poke here for arthurites

Poke feet for athleets foot

Poke Booty for farts

When I was eight, I held anger towards and greatly disliked many people. This voodoo doll helped me get all the pleasure of inflicting harm on those people while not getting me in trouble for it. Double Win!

Step 12: And How Not to Make Enemies

Blending friends from one group with friends from another can be a recipe for making enemies of both of them! For me, it was like swimming in shark-infested waters. Could I figure out how to get to the other side without being eaten?

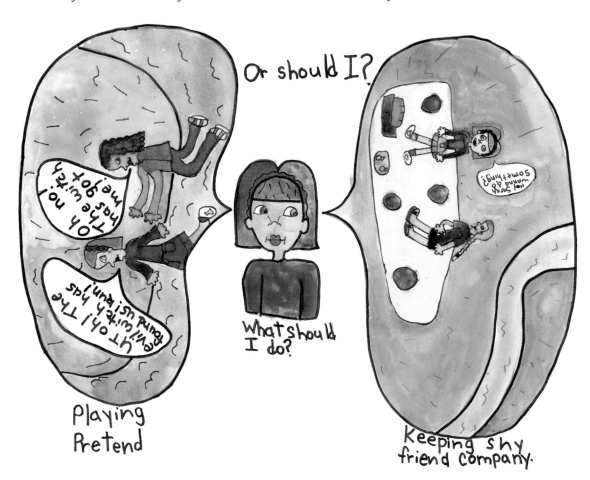

Playing Pretend

Keeping shy friend company.

What should I do?

Despite all my challenges in the realm of human socialization, I did make friends. In fact, I began to belong to a couple of different groups or cliques. I became close friends with one girl who was very reserved and who didn't hang out with my other friends.

I still wanted to be with my other friends, but I felt guilty leaving her alone. This picture showed me that the decision about who to hang out with is hard, but you've got to think of YOU first. If you want, you should go play with the group. It's the other girl's responsibility to overcome her shyness and expand her circle of friends as long as the people around her (like me) are kind.

Step 13: Fear of Bullies

Once you have a bad friend, it may make you afraid of bullies. Don't worry, just stand up for yourself. That's the human thing to do!

Okay, so I was REALLY obsessed with and anxious about bullying when I was eight. The funny thing was, I never was bullied by other kids, just by the evil VOICE in my head. This picture helped me identify causes for bullying as well as a worst case scenario. Though Joan felt embarrassed, she didn't break her arm, go blind, or die. I started to learn that bullying is less about the abuse from the bully, and more about how the bullied stands in the face of it. Bullies only have as much power as their victims give them.

Step 14: Bullying Yourself

Don't torment **yourself** with fears of being left out the way I did.

At age eight, I loved hanging out with Joe, and I considered her to be my **best friend**. Sadly, she already had a best friend named Lea, who had the temperament of a rebellious banshee. I learned that both of their families had agreed to move to Hawaii for a year, and I became deeply **envious** and disheartened. Now there was no way I could ever win the status of being Joe's best friend! This day-mare shows all I thought they'd do together, and all I thought I'd be **left out** of.

Step 15: Mega Cool People

A necessary step to learning to be human is figuring out what makes humans cool and uncool and whether you even care. Essential in any school!

As part of becoming more aware of emotions, I became more aware that some people were **better liked** or revered than others. By drawing this chart about popularity, I developed knowledge about different ranks of the social ladder people belong to, as well as a knowledge of where I might belong.

Perhaps the greatest insight it gave me was that though being on the top rung has much surface appeal, in reality its **tiring** and not very rewarding. Poor Amy... her hand must be tired long before school begins with waving back to all those people. She must suffer in agony for the rest of the day.

What fun!

People who everythinks is cool, and knows.

Hi! Hellooo! Hi there Amy!

Normal cool people

People who know lot's of kids but not everybody

Hehe hehe

Average people

Masses of usual kids that have different personalities but are not cool.

I'm here in the middle

Shy people

People who's voices quiver when they talk

III III.ice haamsters

Different People

People who read during recess.

People who Group together

Some people just do one thing

Rejected People

People who get bullied and who have no friends

Step 16: Cool People to YOU

Figure out the people who really matter!

This meter was part of learning about my **emotions** and the many different types of **friends** around me. It helped me learn that even with the people you like, there are differences in degree of how much you like them and that you can't be best friends unless you have **mutual** feelings of liking or love. FYI, the older friends on this meter are seven, twenty-three, and thirty-something years older than me. I could do the math, but I feel I've shamed enough people already.

Best Friends

Someone you can share delishus secrets with and watch movies and have sleep overs.

Friend

Someone who's almost a best friend but not quite there. You have play dates with them.

Older Friends

Friends that are more than 3 years than you.

Below Friend Level

People you know but arn't friends with.

Faces

You've seen them but don't know them.

Invisable

Like a ghost you've just heard about them never seen them.

Step 17: What Makes a Bad Friend 2

Friendship updated, for more accomplished humans.

Step 18: How to Grow Up

It's one thing being a kid human, an adult human is something else entirely.

On this day in middle school, I was lamenting that I had to grow up. Shelah suggested I make this chart so that I could appreciate the positive parts about being a teen and an adult. I realized that there were many benefits to being both.

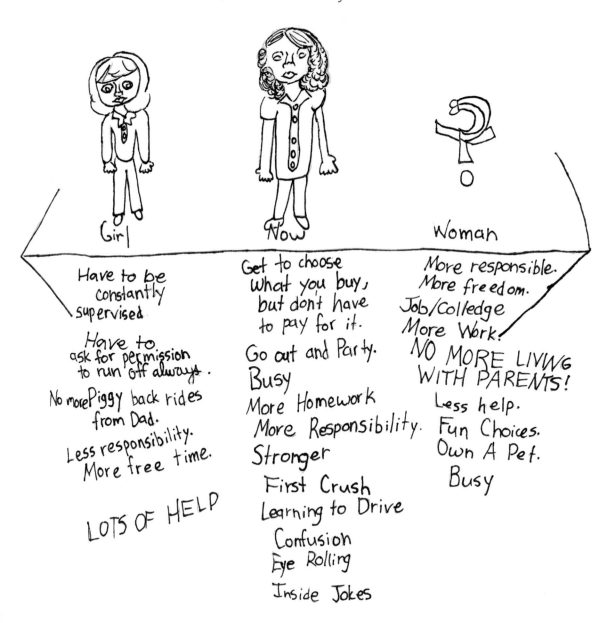

Girl

Have to be constantly supervised

Have to ask for permission to run off always.

No more Piggy back rides from Dad.

Less responsibility. More free time.

LOTS OF HELP

Now

Get to choose what you buy, but don't have to pay for it.

Go out and Party.

Busy

More Homework

More Responsibility.

Stronger

First Crush

Learning to Drive

Confusion

Eye Rolling

Inside Jokes

Woman

More responsible. More freedom.

Job/Colledge

More Work!

NO MORE LIVING WITH PARENTS!

Less help.

Fun Choices.

Own A Pet.

Busy

Step 19: Consequences

A tough part of being an older human is learning these kinds of lessons.

I was on an airplane and having just quenched my thirst, I put my bottle of water back inside my backpack. Unfortunately the cap wasn't screwed on tightly enough, and the water spilled on everything inside my backpack, including many pages of the book I had in there. My mom reprimanded me for being so careless. I felt angry that she'd reprimanded me as well as guilty that I hadn't taken better care of my stuff. To repress that guilt, I tried to convince myself that Mom had way overreacted, and that she just maliciously wanted to irk me. This picture helped me realize that she hadn't overreacted and that she never had any evil schemes in mind. All she wanted me to do was learn a lesson and close the darn water bottle.

Step 20: Juggling

Growing up means more freedom, but lots more responsibility. I'm still figuring this one out.

   When I entered my freshman year of high school, I did not expect any sort of circus training to come in handy. However, I soon found out juggling was necessary for my survival because I had an unrelenting **tidal wave** of work. All the things that I juggle in the picture created a lot of stress. Juggling stress was like being a ring master who had to juggle all the different circus acts while dealing with the 800-pound-gorilla in the room, but once I learned to do that, I was more able to handle all the other balls.

Step 21: Mature or Immature Human?

Peer pressure can make this really hard to figure out.

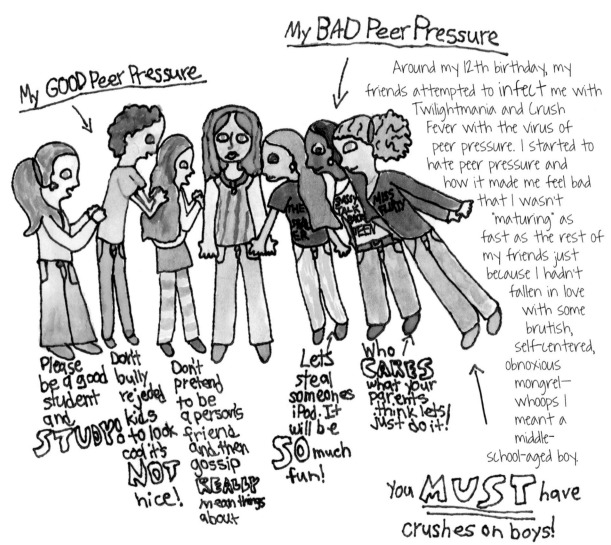

In this picture I began to explore both good and bad kinds of peer pressure, as well as how to build **immunity** to Twilightmania, Crush Fever, and all other forms of Peer-Pressure-Germs that can infect you.

Step 22: Express Yourself!

It took a lot of hard work, but now I can show people how I feel and understand those feelings better myself.

Outside On A Good Day

Inside On A Good Day

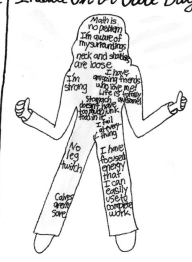

Math is no problem
I'm aware of my surroundings
neck and shoulders are loose
I have amazing friends who love me!
I'm strong
Life is totally awesome!
Stomach doesn't have too much junk food in it
I fail at everything
No leg twitch
I have focused energy that I can easily use to complete work
Calves aren't sore

Outside On A Bad Day

Inside On A Bad Day

Fetal position for protection and comfort

I updated the "Inside And Outside" picture to fit myself as a teenager. Okay, I might have stretched reality a tiny bit with the Outside On A Bad Day picture, but it was the most fun to draw.

Step 23: Human or Alien?

After all this, I'm just as human — and alien — as everyone else!
I really do belong on this planet!

Afterword
By Shelah Moss

One sunny day in August I went to meet a new client. I had been working with autistic children for about a decade using a developmental approach based on Floortime. When I got to the client's house I met an adorable four year old girl, Florida, with a mop of hair and bright eyes that saw the world in black and white and red. The black and white part were the rules and rigidity that she lived by. The red was there because she had decided that red was her favorite color so she believed that her clothes should be red, her food should be red whenever possible, and she would only use the color red for her art projects.

Her mother told me her history. She had been diagnosed with autism at age three. The diagnostics tests showed that she was mentally retarded as well as autistic. As soon as the diagnosis was confirmed, Florida began a regimen of speech therapy, occupational therapy, ABA (Applied Behavioral Analysis) and enrolled in a typical preschool with a one-on-one aide. Her mother told me that while she was not complaining about the therapy, she was concerned about the lack of developmental progress. I was there specifically to teach her daughter how to pretend. I told her that I had done it before. The mother gave me a skeptical look, but she and Florida's father hired me. I thought it was my confidence that won them over. I later found out that what had really convinced them was that during our session Florida painted a picture using all the colors on her easel without crying for the first time. That started my long journey with Florida and her wonderful parents.

The ABA therapists soon faded away and a core team consisting of me, Sarah Homewood, her aide and therapist, Maggie Newman, an extraordinary occupational therapist, and Florida's parents was formed. When Florida was quite young, social skills and developing through play were the primary focus. Somehow Florida's mother convinced the other mothers from her preschool to bring their children for one-hour play dates to work on her social skills. Those parents were generous with their time and their compassion for Florida. Hopefully they know today how much those hours of play helped Florida to develop friendships and meaningful relationships.

As Florida grew, it became evident that she had many issues other than autism. She enrolled in a private kindergarten. When that didn't work out she was enrolled in kindergarten at her local school. When that didn't work out, her parents asked the team if we would homeschool Florida. Her mother made sure that we addressed each issue. When it was obvious that Florida had dysgraphia, (an impairment that affects the ability to write letters), we all did handwriting practice every day. When it was discovered that Florida had a reading disability, I learned how to be a reading specialist, and Florida did the Lindamood-Bell "Seeing Stars" program every session with me. When her visual-spatial disability became obvious, Sarah went with her to vision therapy and then did vision exercises with her every day. Maggie came three times a week to work on fine and gross motor skills. The whole time that we were working on these core skills, her autism was never forgotten. Every session included social skills and learning through play. As Maggie said, "A lot of therapy hours went into that girl."

Having an effective team working with Florida over the years was crucial to her success, but it would not have been nearly as effective if Florida herself had not been motivated to change. When she was younger, she was not really aware that she was so different from other children. After her experience with kindergarten, she was sure that she was different, but she did not know why. She figured it out herself when she was seven. She was watching a television show about service dogs. One of the people featured was a severely autistic boy who needed a service dog to help him get through the day. The boy was far more autistic than Florida, but she recognized herself in that boy. She asked if she, too, was autistic and that was when she became aware of her diagnosis. What followed was a year of grief. Florida needed to work through what it meant to be autistic and what she wanted to do about it. Many tears and tantrums later, Florida decided that she wanted to work hard to overcome those parts of her autism that kept her shunted aside from the rest of the world. It was that decision that made change truly possible.

The work that you see in this book started during that year of discovering what being autistic meant to Florida. She is a gifted artist and writer so using art seemed like an obvious tool to help her work through understanding what, to her, were foreign concepts. Each picture represents hours where we discussed or read about or role-played different scenarios. The pictures represent eight years of growth.

Today Florida attends an academically rigorous private high school. When her parents enrolled her, they did not tell the administration that she was autistic. They were not trying to hide that fact, they just did not feel that it was relevant. Despite that early diagnosis of mental retardation, Florida is taking AP classes. Her friends know that she is autistic but they don't seem to care. It's a beautiful human world that she lives in now, and I am glad to be part of it.

About the Author

Due to a glitch in the time-space continuum, Florida Frenz wound up on the wrong planet. On the planet she should have been on, everyone is autistic. When no work needs to get done, everyone spends their time flapping, doodling, and spinning. However, Earth has become a home to Florida, and she has discovered many Earthlings can be fun and nice. Florida especially loves Earthling kids, whose brains are very receptive to new ideas, and her friends, who like her, may be from other planets, but are adapting fabulously to their lives on Earth. She would also like to thank all of those who help her to remain incognito and support her right to act different when she chooses.

31901055556361